THE PEASANT POETS OF SOLENTINAME

Poetry is born in a frangipani flower
where red butterflies suck the nectar.
Poetry is what a pair of lovers
say to each other.
Poetry is more delicate
than the moon's reflection in the lake.
A perfect poem is like the Revolution.

Juan Agudelo (aged 7)

KATABASIS

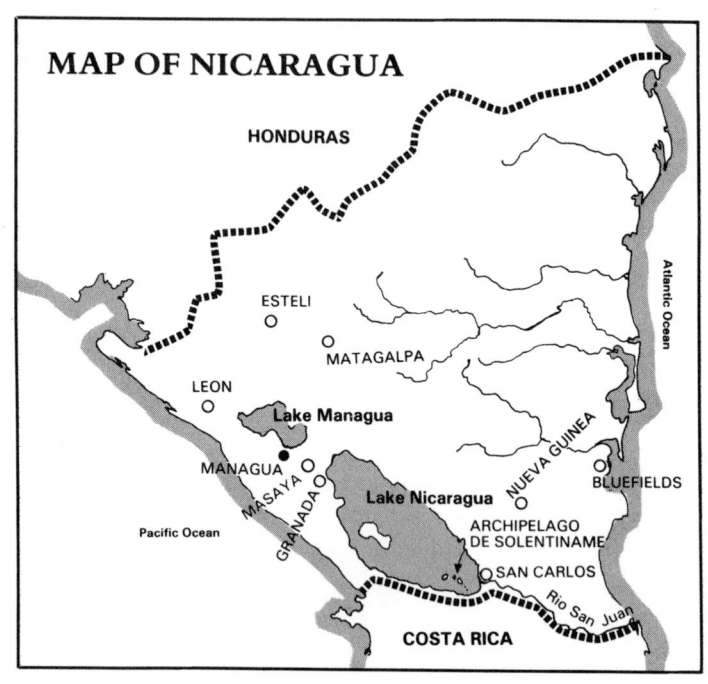
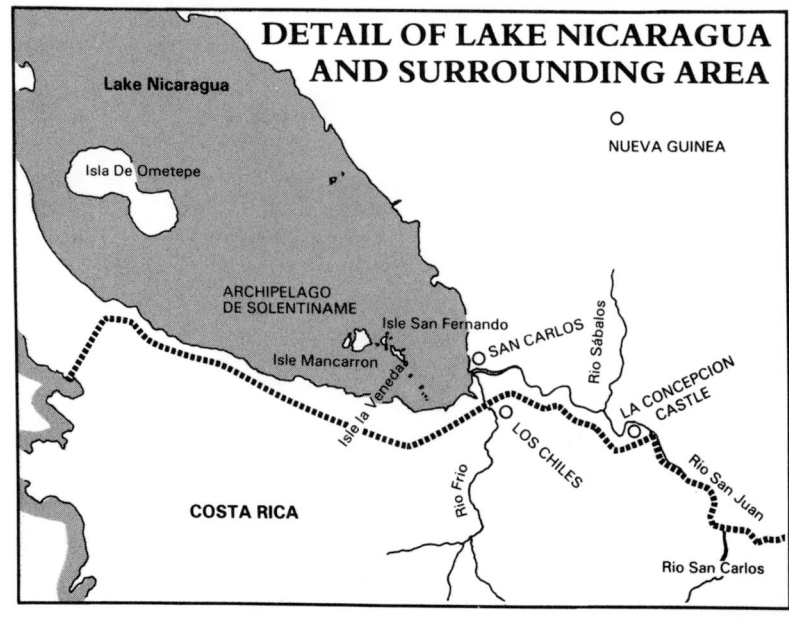

THE PEASANT POETS OF SOLENTINAME

TRANSLATED BY PETER WRIGHT

First Published 1991 by KATABASIS,
10 St Martins Close, London NW1 0HR
Original Spanish language edition: Managua 1980
Copyright remains with the authors 1991
Translation copyright: Peter Wright 1991

KATABASIS is grateful for the assistance of the Arts Council of Great Britain and Greater London Arts.

British Library Cataloguing in Publication Data

    The Peasant Poets of Solentiname
    1. Nicaragua
    I. Wright, Peter
    861-00808687285

    ISBN 0-904872-15-7

The front cover painting of Solentiname is by the poet Myriam Guevara
The section title illustrations are by Anna Mieke Lumsden
Cover designed by Dale Russell, Boldface
Designed and Typeset by BOLDFACE, 17a Clerkenwell Road, London EC1 (071-253 2014)
Printed by SHORT RUN PRESS (0296 631075)

CONTENTS

INTRODUCTION   1

ISLANDS IN THE LAKE
Miro el reventar de las olas/	Elvis Chavarría	8
I Watch the Waves Breaking		
Vida en Solentiname/Life in Solentiname	Dónald Guevara	10
Noche/Night	Pedro Pablo Meneses	12
El malinche/The Flame-Tree	Juan Agudelo	14
Los garrobos/Lizards	Eddy Chavarría	16
Chicharras, güises, gavilanes/	Elvis Chavarría	18
Cicadas, Flycatchers, Sparrow-Hawks		

THE SEASONS
El malinche rojo/The Red Flame-Tree	Pedro Pablo Meneses	20
Invierno/Winter	Eddy Chavarría	22
Invierno/Winter	Elvis Chavarría	22
Verano/Summer	Elvis Chavarría	24
Chubascos de febrero/February Squalls	Bosco Centeno	26
Cuando los árboles . . . /When the Trees . . .	Eddy Chavarría	28

CREATURES
Las garzas/Herons	Alejandro Guevara	30
El garrobo/The Lizard	Bosco Centeno	32
Todos los pájaros/A Congregation of Love	Natalia Sequeira	34
Los vacunos/Cattle	Dónald Guevara	36
Amor en el campo/Love in the Countryside	Elvis Chavarría	38

FAMILY AND FRIENDS
Feliz/Happiness	Jonny Chavarría	40
A mi padre/To My Father	Felipe Peña	42
Recuerdo/A Memory	Gloria Guevara	44
Es casi ya de noche/It's Almost Night	Iván Guevara	46
El amor es como la mata de frijol/	Iván Guevara	48
Love is like a Bean-Plant		
Con el pelo alborotado/With my Hair all Tumbled	Nubia Arcia	50

POLITICS AND REVOLUTION
Ayer pasé por este ranchito/	Esperanza Guevara	52
Yesterday I Passed by this Little Hut		
Plagas/Pests	Felipe Peña	54
El pueblo en miseria/The People in Poverty	Gloria Guevara	56
Campesino/Peasant	Jonny Chavarría	58
San Carlos	Elvis Chavarría	60
La Revolución es . . . /The Revolution is . . .	Juan Agudelo	62

THE LIBERATION STRUGGLE

Blanca estoy triste/I am Sad, Blanca	Felipe Peña	64
Vos creés/You Suppose	Felipe Peña	66
Despedida del padre/Farewell to my Father	Felipe Peña	68
Después de la emboscada/After the Ambush	Iván Guevara	70
Tenle miedo a los poetas tirano/ Walk in Dread of Poets, Tyrant	Bosco Centeno	72
Hermano guardia perdoná/Brother Soldier	Bosco Centeno	74
Sudorosos y enlodados/Sweaty and Muddy	Bosco Centeno	76
En la noche confundidos/Obscured by the Night	Bosco Centeno	78
A mis cuatro hijos en la montaña/ To my Four Sons in the Mountains	Olivia Silva	80
El hijo/A Son	Gloria Guevara	82
El guerrillero/The Guerrillero	Gloria Guevara	84

THE ASSAULT ON SAN CARLOS

En Nicaragua el gran asalto/ In Nicaragua the Great Assault	Pedro Pablo Meneses	86
12 de octubre de 1977/The 12th of October 1977	Olivia Silva	88
Cuando el asalto/At the Time of the Assault	Olivia Silva	90
Cuando los muchachos de Solentiname . . . / When the Young Men and Women of Solentiname . . .	Elena Pineda	92
Recuerdo aquella madrugada/A Dawn Memory	Nubia Arcia	94
Al Chato Medrano/To Chato Medrano	Myriam Guevara	96
Después del combate/After the Battle	Myriam Guevara	98

CAPTIVITY AND EXILE

En Solentiname/In Solentiname	Olivia Silva	100
A mi Nicaragua/To My Nicaragua	Iván Guevara	102
En Solentiname/In Solentiname	Iván Guevara	104
La iglesia sola/The Empty Church	Iván Guevara	106
Visita de una amiga/Visit from a Friend	Felipe Peña	108
Nostalgia desde la cárcel/Homesickness in Prison	Felipe Peña	110
A Esperanza mi mujer/To my Wife Esperanza	Bosco Centeno	112
Solentiname	Bosco Centeno	114

INDEX OF POETS AND NOTES   118

INTRODUCTION

The archipelago of Solentiname – thirty-eight islands and islets – lies in the extreme south-east corner of the immense Lake of Nicaragua, opposite the little town of San Carlos, departmental capital of the Río San Juan region. It is an area of singular beauty, with tropical forest running down to the lake on both sides.

But under the long reign of the Somoza family it was also an area of extreme poverty, of large estates and landless peasants, with 96 per cent adult illiteracy, life expectancy the lowest in the land, and infant mortality the highest. Most of the population lived in a sad state of neglect and deprivation.

San Carlos was – and is – virtually inaccessible from the main centres of the country for most of the year except by ferry across nearly a hundred miles of a sometimes turbulent lake. Solentiname lies another hour away by motor-launch, and during the dictatorship was the most neglected part of the region. There was no school, no doctor, not even a resident priest: politicians and the Church paid only occasional visits, to offer bribes in return for votes, or to preach religion of the 'pray and obey' variety, in the words of Olivia Silva, one of the poets (and mother of half a dozen more). The peasants wrung a meagre living out of the arid land or the lake, taking their beans, rice, maize or fish by water to San Carlos, where (Olivia again) 'all we got was just enough to keep us in poverty'.

Yet it was on one of these islands that at the end of 1976 there began a remarkable flowering of poetry, written almost exclusively by a score or so of peasant men and women – most of them not long out of their teens – and even a few children. They continued to write during the strife-torn years before the triumph of the Sandinista revolution, sometimes in the heat of battle, often from exile in Costa Rica. In 1980 an anthology of their work was published by the Ministry of Culture in Managua, and it is from there that these poems are taken.

With all the disadvantages they suffered, how did these peasant men and women – *campesinos* – come to write?

The story goes back to early 1966, when most of the poets were still children. It was then that the recently ordained priest, Ernesto Cardenal, (now forty years old) arrived with two companions on the island of Mancarrón, the largest in the archipelago, with the aim of setting up a small Catholic community. Two years in a Trappist monastery in

Kentucky, under the spiritual guidance of the American radical theologian, Thomas Merton; and six years studying for the priesthood in Mexico and Colombia, had brought him into contact with liberation theologians, whose radical doctrines were by now being fiercely debated throughout Latin America. Before becoming a priest, however, Cardenal was already widely known as a poet, though censorship under Somoza often prevented him from publishing in Nicaragua. As a young man he had studied literature in Mexico and the US, and was deeply influenced by radical poets like Alberti and Lorca from Spain, the Chilean Pablo Neruda and the Peruvian César Vallejo. Through such reading he was already encountering the influence of Marx, whose ideas appealed to him for much the same reasons as those of liberation theology; in the course of time he would attempt to make a working synthesis of these two ways of looking at the world.

Growing up under the Somoza regime, Cardenal had always felt a deep hatred for the dictator, whom he denounced in some of his earliest poems. After returning to Nicaragua in 1950, he became involved in an insurrectionary movement, and in 1954 took part in a conspiracy to overthrow Somoza. The conspiracy was betrayed, some of the leading conspirators were executed, and Cardenal was forced to go into hiding.

It was soon after this that he decided to enter the monastery, but he never lost his profound interest in history, society and politics, which were to constitute the central themes of the poetry he had still to write. By the time he reached Solentiname, the three main strands of his thought – theology, poetry and politics – were already intertwined.

Writing twelve years later, Cardenal defined his theological and political position. He had gone to Solentiname, he said, to found a small contemplative community. 'Contemplation means union with God. We soon realised that union with God meant in the first place union with the peasants who lived, poor and neglected, scattered along the shores of the archipelago. Contemplation also led us to a political commitment: it led us to revolution... Thomas Merton had told me that in Latin America the contemplative man could not stand aside from political struggle. At first we would have preferred a non-violent revolution... but later we came to realise that in present-day Nicaragua that is not practicable.'

★ ★ ★

'Ernesto immediately began to take an interest in the community,' testified one of the islanders, 'and with his sermons to awaken people to the way human beings *could* live.' These 'sermons' were, in fact, dialogues, initiated by Ernesto after mass every Sunday, either in the little adobe church or seated in a circle outside. One of the younger members of the congregation – many of the older ones were illiterate – would read a text from one of the gospels; it would then be discussed and interpreted, verse by verse, by the whole group. The consistent message elicited from the text was the central one of liberation theology – in Ernesto's words: 'The news of the coming of the Kingdom of God – that is, the establishment on earth of a just society, without exploiters or exploited, with all goods held in common, as in the society of the early Christians.' It was in these meetings that the peasants, old and young, received their 'awakening'.

There is no space here to give a detailed account of other changes brought about by Cardenal in Solentiname. In ten years the islanders were transformed from a thin scattering of isolated and illiterate peasants into something like a close-knit, self-aware and purposeful community. They had a school, a library, a museum. Between them they built kilns and a large craft workshop, and many of them became increasingly involved in crafts such as pottery, wood-carving and sculpture. But the greatest discovery was the apparently natural talent so many of them had for painting.

Painting was to become the first glory of Solentiname. Soon after his arrival Ernesto saw some attractively decorated gourds, and diagnosed a potential painter. He provided materials, and the peasant artist proved indeed to have considerable skills. The sale of one of his pictures in Managua led to his example being followed, and it was only a matter of time before large numbers of colourful peasant paintings were being produced. With some of the craft work, they were exhibited and sold, at first in the capital, and in the years to come in the art centres of the US and Europe. The income from these sales enabled the islanders to improve the quality of their lives in various ways (getting medical treatment, buying farm animals and so on), but more importantly this genuinely creative activity raised them enormously in their own estimation, and together with the impact of liberation theology enabled them to express their expanding vision of the world. As they became aware of the growth of active opposition to the tyranny of Somoza, many of the paintings depicted the struggle for political liberation in terms of the New Testament story, showing Jesus, for example, simultaneously as the crucified Christ and as a Nicaraguan guerrilla fighter.

Surprisingly, the one cultural area which Cardenal felt unable to open up with the community was his own speciality, poetry. It was some ten years after the foundation of the community that he was prompted by the Costa Rican poet, Mayra Jiménez, to think about this anomaly. There was a flourishing group of painters and craft workers in Solentiname, and he himself was a poet: why no poets? He replied that 'he didn't know how to go about it'. Painting, yes. The Gospel, yes. But poetry . . . ! However, he knew that Mayra had had previous experience with children and adolescents, and he invited her to go to Solentiname and see what could be done. She accepted.

She arrived on a Sunday in November, 1976. During mass Cardenal announced her, and said she had come to talk about poetry: any one interested could stay behind after mass. She had expected three or four; to her surprise about thirty stayed. She asked them if they were familiar with Ernesto's poetry: they said they had never heard it. He had been living with them for ten years, and he had never read them poetry of any kind! They didn't even know he was a poet – they always thought of him as El Padre Ernesto. She began by reading them some of his poetry, which they then commented on: they were very enthusiastic.

Later she read them poetry by other Nicaraguan poets, including José Coronel Urtecho, Ernesto's uncle, who lived just across the Costa Rican frontier in Los Chiles, and had several times visited Solentiname. She extended the reading to the work of poets from other countries, sometimes in translation; they particularly liked Chinese poetry, which Ernesto translated from English (he did not attend many of the sessions, but stayed in his *rancho* writing: he wrote a great deal of poetry during the Solentiname years, and also compiled an anthology of Nicaraguan poetry).

Without any prompting from Mayra, these *campesinos* began to write poetry themselves, on topics from their own lives, their own surroundings. In her preface to the Solentiname anthology, which she edited, Mayra describes what happened in these poetry workshops.

'We would read and discuss them (the poets) from early afternoon until sunset. As we were on one of the islands of Solentiname, and there were few families living on it, I could see, far across the lake, the little boats coming from other islands, bringing young lads and girls, and children too, to the poetry sessions. I never asked any one to write. Poetry flowed naturally and quickly from them... The first poems they wrote were discussed between the writer and me, but always in the presence of other members of the group. We then started a group discussion, every one saying what was good and what seemed not so good. Sometimes the writer would defend his or her position, at other times making changes, and more than once deleting the original version and starting again... The important thing to stress is that (these peasants) had poetry in them, and that, in Ernesto's words, it appeared as if by a miracle.' She also stresses that the writing of poetry in these circumstances was essentially a collective experience, and that the product was 'a peasant poetry, of the people and for the people, and therefore an eminently social, political and human product. In short, a poetry of revolution and living testimony.'

Though Ernesto took little part in the workshops, there is a significant relationship between Mayra Jiménez's approach to poetry and his own ideas on the subject. In his preface to the anthology mentioned above, he sets out his criteria for his choice of poems. The first is literary worth, but it is not the only one. Literature, he says, must be in the service of humanity; thus poetry must be political (though not propagandist). It should be 'exteriorist', that is, 'poetry created from images from the external world, the world that we see and feel... objective poetry: narrative and anecdotal, composed of the elements of real life and of concrete things, with proper names and precise details and exact information and figures and facts and words. In short, it is *impure* poetry.' Some examples: the engine of a plane shot down by guerrillas; a steamy, gnat-ridden afternoon in a little port, with Somoza's portrait hanging in a grubby office; adolescent love, with twist and rock and visits to the cinema; the secret journeys of Che Guevara; the smile of the check-out girl in a supermarket. Readers will judge for themselves to what extent these categories are valid, and whether the poems in this book belong to them.

These peaceful and creative activities were soon to be harshly interrupted. Cardenal had for some years been in close contact with the Sandinista leaders, and by 1976 was effectively one of them. When Mayra had been in Solentiname for some months, he received information that a guerrilla operation was planned for October, and that he and Mayra should leave for Costa Rica. The forces of resistance to

Somoza had for some time been gathering strength, and many of the islanders were keen to translate their feelings of solidarity with the movement into action; some had begun to train with the Sandinista guerrillas on the mainland. On 13th October a Solentiname contingent took part in a combined assault on the National Guard barracks in San Carlos. It was a bold and hazardous operation. A tiny force of men and women, hastily trained, inexperienced, and with only a few antiquated weapons among them (not even a weapon each), attacked well-armed and experienced troops in the relative security of their own headquarters. Alejandro Guevara entered the barracks when there was nobody left but dead and wounded soldiers. He was going to set fire to the barracks but did not do so out of consideration for the wounded National Guards. Although the element of surprise had enabled the guerrillas to inflict heavy casualties in the early phases of the operation, because of poor communications other guerrilla forces failed to arrive in time, and Somoza was able to drive the attacking columns back by sending in his air force. Soon afterwards he dispatched a special National Guard contingent to carry out savage reprisals against the Solentiname community.

At least ten of the poets took part in the assault. Five of them belonged to the Guevara family: Alejandro, Iván, Dónald, and their sisters Myriam and Gloria. Their mother, Olivia Silva (married to Julio Guevara), had been evacuated from Solentiname with their sister Esperanza on the day before the battle. Others were Felipe Peña, Bosco Centeno (who married Esperanza), Elvis Chavarría, Nubia Arcia (who married Alejandro), and Pedro Pablo Meneses. Elena Pineda was involved in evacuating children from the islands.

Felipe Peña, Elvis Chavarría and Dónald Guevara were captured during the retreat. The last two were tortured and killed by the National Guard. Felipe was released on 22nd August, 1978, as a result of the storming of the Palace in Managua by the Sandinistas; but after a brief period of rest in Costa Rica rejoined the guerrillas in Nueva Guinea. In May 1979 he was killed in action in that area whilst trying to save a wounded comrade. Many of the survivors went into exile in Costa Rica, some until the Sandinista victory, others to return to the struggle when it became possible. The poets continued to write.

After the final defeat of Somoza in July, 1979, the Sandinista government launched a massive and successful literacy campaign, coordinated by Ernesto Cardenal's brother Fernando. At about the same time, Ernesto inaugurated nation-wide poetry workshops: he invited Mayra to carry on the work she had begun in Solentiname.

★ ★ ★

These poets write very little about their inward feelings: they have, perhaps unwittingly, followed Ernesto's 'exteriorist' guidance. The language of their poems is certainly direct and spare, without studied symbolism or rhetorical flourishes. They write about things seen and heard and remembered, and their observations are unemphatic, matter-of-fact. Poems written before their participation in the armed struggle are about their surroundings: the lake, fish, lizards, birds, cattle, storms, the seasons; and about friendship, love, children, (and surprisingly seldom about poverty and hardship). They say little about the beauty of this 'almost Paradise', as Ernesto called it: they simply show it to us. After October, 1977 there is, inevitably, a thematic change: now they write about the armed struggle; about the brutal destruction of their beloved community by the National Guard; about the pain of separation and exile; and about their hopes for a new life through the victory of the Revolution. Their contribution to that victory in 1979 was not negligible. Despite the electoral setback of February 1990, their faith and hope in the Revolution are very much alive.

Peter Wright
December 1990

TRANSLATOR'S ACKNOWLEDGMENTS

Many people, both here and in Nicaragua, have given me encouragement and friendly criticism. My thanks to them, and particularly to Robert Pring-Mill, for useful background material and some valuable introductions; to Mayra Jiménez and Olivia Silva, with whom I had long and fruitful discussions; to Ernesto Cardenal who warmly encouraged the project; to Dinah Livingstone, a fellow translator into English whose criticism I have particularly cherished because she is also a poet; and to my family, and especially to my wife Brigit, for their constant interest and support. Any shortcomings in the translation are solely my responsibility.

P.K.W.

MIRO EL REVENTAR DE LAS OLAS

Miro el reventar de las olas.
Una bandada de garzas pasa.
Tres cocas como damas
sentadas en una roca.
Un bote pasa como pluma
entre las olas.

Elvis Chavarría

ISLANDS IN THE LAKE

I WATCH THE WAVES BREAKING

I watch the waves breaking:
a flight of herons passes overhead.
Three white ibises sit like so many ladies
on a rock.
A boat bobs among the waves
like a feather.

VIDA EN SOLENTINAME

Solentiname
pequeño archipiélago del lago
lugar donde el poeta
da sabor a sus poesías.
A causa de su silencio inmenso
sólo se escucha el güir güir de los patos chanchos,
el canto de los güises
y el clarín de los zanates
y el escándalo de los tijules
cuando la chocalla llega a sus pichones
el romper de las olas contra las empedradas costas
que dan origen y final a cada isla
donde las tortugas pasan y disfrutan de los calientes rayos
    del sol.
Solo miro y escucho un bote de remos
que a lo lejos alguien, extraño, pudiera creer que es
alguna lechuga de río que va a la deriva
y es mi querida Mimí
que va de pesca.

Dónald Guevara

LIFE IN SOLENTINAME

Solentiname –
little archipelago in the lake,
the place where the poet
gives flavour to his poems.
In the measureless silence
only the sound of birds can be heard:
the quack, quack of grubby ducks,
the cry of the flycatchers,
the bugle call of the grackle,
and the uproar of the waterfowl
when the *chocalla* flies in to its chicks;
the lapping of the waves against the stony shores
which begin and end each island,
where the tortoises come to enjoy the warm sun.
I see and hear nothing but a rowing-boat,
which from a distance a stranger might think
was just some river-plant drifting down,
but which is really my beloved Mimí
going fishing.

NOCHE

La noche con una luna llena
reflejada en el lago calmo;
el lago dorado y plateado.
Veo un cuaco
cazando sardinas.
Un coro de sapos cantando.
El alegre canto de los pocoyos
diciendo: Jodido, rejodido
brincando de una piedra a otra.
La lechuza pasa silbando.
Sopla un viento fresco.

Pedro Pablo Meneses

NIGHT

Night.
The full moon
reflected in the still lake,
the lake streaked with gold and silver.
I can see a night-heron
fishing for sardines.
Toads are singing in chorus.
The night-jars hop from stone to stone,
singing happily: Screw you, I'll do you.
An owl flies hooting by.
A fresh breeze blows.

EL MALINCHE

En la isla de Mancarrón
hay un malinche frondoso
con las ramas llenas de flores
de color amarillo, negro y anaranjado;
y unas mariposas
anaranjadas, negras y amarillas
chupando miel dulce,
y el güis pecho amarillo, espalda café
comiendo mariposas.

*Juan Agudelo
(aged 7)*

THE FLAME-TREE

On the island of Mancarrón
is a leafy flame-tree,
with branches full of flowers,
yellow, black and orange;
and there are butterflies,
orange, black and yellow,
sucking the sweet honey;
and a flycatcher,
with yellow breast and coffee-coloured back –
eating butterflies.

LOS GARROBOS

Los garrobos a la punta
de un palo seco
calientan en el sol de mediodía.
Los mangos y naranjos
se mecen
continuamente
con el zumbar del viento
y allá en la punta de una isla
las olas se rompen donde
más adelante
en una ensenada muy mansa
se encuentra un ranchito
de paja,
muy natural,
que sirve para pintar la humildad
de sus habitantes.

Eddy Chavarría

LIZARDS

Lizards on the top
of a dried-up tree-trunk
bask in the mid-day sun.
Mango and orange trees
sway
ceaselessly
to the murmur of the wind.
And there at the tip of an island
the waves are breaking and
a little beyond
in a quiet creek
is a little hut
made of straw,
very simple,
which serves to illustrate
the humble ways
of the people who live in it.

CHICHARRAS, GÜISES, GAVILANES

Chicharras, güises, gavilanes
cantan al anochecer.
Loras pasan volando a su dormitorio,
allá en una loma.
Entra la noche.
Pocoyos, lechuzas, ranas, grillos;
un martín-peña con su ronco cántico.
Alberto en su rancho dice: – va a haber sequía.
La noche transcurre quieta.
De repente gallos cantan.
Amanece.
Y se oye el trinar de todos los pájaros.
Juan dice: – Compadre ¿oyó anoche cantar el punco?
– Sí compadre. – Entonces, no hay que sembrar.

Elvis Chavarría

CICADAS, FLYCATCHERS, SPARROW-HAWKS

Cicadas, flycatchers, sparrow-hawks,
all sing at dusk.
Parrots fly to their sleeping-places
over there on the hill.
Night steals in.
Night-jars, owls, frogs, crickets;
a heron with its hoarse chant.
From his hut Alberto says: 'There's going to be a drought.'
The night slips quietly by.
Suddenly the cocks begin to crow.
It is dawn.
And you can hear the carolling of all the birds.
Juan says: '*Compadre*, did you hear the bittern call last night?'
'Yes, *compadre*.' 'Then it's not time to sow.'

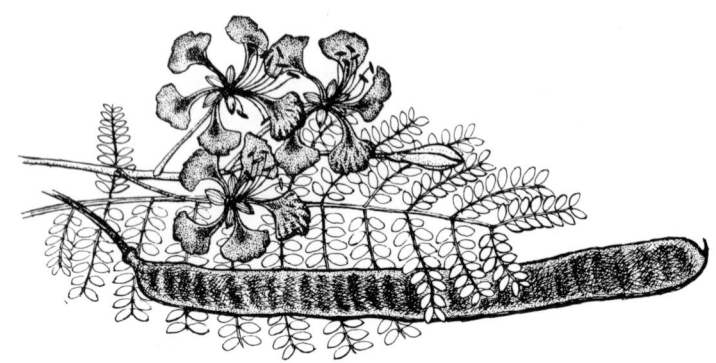

EL MALINCHE ROJO

El malinche rojo
el cortés de La Cigüeña florecido amarillo,
las tortugas subiendo a desovar en noche de luna llena.
Cantan los pocoyos,
los llanos quemados,
los venados bebiendo agua en la costa seca.
Han llegado las primeras lluvias,
olor a tierra mojada, los güises cantan alegres,
es mayo en Solentiname.

Pedro Pablo Meneses

THE SEASONS

THE RED FLAME-TREE

Red flame-tree.
Golden trumpet-tree in flower on the island of La Cigüeña.
Turtles coming ashore to lay their eggs at full moon.
Night-jars singing.
The plains burnt dry.
Deer drinking along the arid shore.
The first rains have fallen.
There's a smell of damp earth. Flycatchers sing joyfully.
It's May in Solentiname.

INVIERNO

El invierno viene cantando
con sus chaparrones y vendavales.
Viste caminos árboles y montañas
impresionando con su colorido.
El lago se traga los corrales de piedra,
las costas se estrechan.
Las tardes son grises, silenciosas.
Las noches son negras.

Eddy Chavarría

★ ★ ★

Las 'viudas' cantan en todos los potreros
anunciando verano.
En las ramas de los maderos
con su pico negro y su pecho amarillo
cantan y cantan toda la mañana.

Elvis Chavarría

WINTER

Winter comes singing in
with its gales and rainstorms.
It covers the roads, the trees and the mountains,
exciting us with its colours.
The lake swallows up the stone fish-traps
on its narrowing shores.
The afternoons are grey and silent.
The nights are black.

★ ★ ★

The widow-birds are singing in all the meadows,
heralding the summer.
In the branches of the trees,
yellow-breasted, black-beaked,
they sing and sing the morning through.

VERANO

Se mira el rosado de la flor del madero,
el rojo naranja del elemeque;
el correr de la iguana;
amarillo intenso del poroporo,
verde frondoso del sonzonate.
Los llanos ya secos;
las tortugas ya están subiendo a desovar.
Olor a pinol de iguana en cada rancho.
Los pescados secos colgando en los patios.
El sol fuerte, el monte seco.
Las guatuzas bajo los palos de coyol.
Los gorriones brincando de flor en flor.
Es el tiempo de los jocotes, mangos, marañones,
y del almíbar en Solentiname.

Elvis Chavarría

SUMMER

Rose-pink flowers on the tree,
orange-red on the *elemeque*;
iguanas scurrying;
wild cotton – rich yellow;
buckthorn – leafy green.
The plains are already dry;
tortoises are coming in to lay their eggs.
In every hut there's a smell of maize julap
with a whiff of iguana.
Dried fish are hung up in the patios.
The sun is hot, the hillsides are dry.
Agoutis run about beneath the coyol palm.
Humming-birds skim over the flowers.
It's the season for eating *jocotes*, mangos, cashew nuts,
and drinking syrup in Solentiname.

CHUBASCOS DE FEBRERO

Chubascos de febrero violentos
las garzas y los patos buscan en vano un remanso donde pescar
los botecitos aparecen y desaparecen
y las golondrinas volando sobre las olas sin mojarse
el vuelo de las garzas llevadas por el viento
y el cielo como un rastrojo lejano en llamas.

Bosco Centeno

FEBRUARY SQUALLS

In February's violent squalls
herons and ducks search vainly for a quiet pool to fish in.
Little boats come and go.
Swallows stay dry as they skim the waves.
Herons are borne away on the wind,
and the sky is like a distant field of burning stubble.

CUANDO LOS ÁRBOLES EMPIEZAN A BOTAR LAS HOJAS

Cuando los árboles empiezan a botar las hojas
y el lago a consecuencia de los agotadores soles
comienza a secar,
y cuando los caminos se convierten
en callejones polvosos,
y cuando en cada rancho
al pasar cerca
se siente el olor a rosquillas calientes,
empanaditas de maíz,
es cuando en Solentiname
ha llegado la Semana Santa.

Eddy Chavarría

WHEN THE TREES BEGIN TO SHED THEIR LEAVES

When the trees begin to shed their leaves,
and days of gruelling sunshine
begin to dry up the lake;
and when the highways
become dusty tracks;
and when from every hut you pass
comes the smell of hot rolls
of maize bread –
then it is Holy Week in Solentiname.

LAS GARZAS

Las garzas grandes
blancas y elegantes
pescando todo el día.
Protestan y hasta pelean cuando otra
pesca en su costa favorita.
Cada sardina es un viaje al nido
porque en su estrecho estómago
caben dos
una de su alimento y otra para
un pichón.

Una garza de largo
se puede confundir con una virgen.

Alejandro Guevara

CREATURES

HERONS

Tall herons,
white and elegant,
fishing all day long.
They grumble and even brawl when others
fish on their favourite beach.
Every sardine means a trip to the nest,
for in their slender stomachs
there is room for only two,
one for themselves, and one
for a chick.

From a distance a heron
could be mistaken for a statue of the Virgin.

EL GARROBO

El gran garrobo lapo
que vivía en la cumbrita
del palo de ojoche
y que se confundía siempre
entre sus hojas,
al fin lo pude coger
y mañana
lo comeremos
en rico pinol.

Bosco Centeno

THE LIZARD

There was a big green lizard
that lived at the very top
of the *ojoche* tree
and was invisible among its leaves.
At last I have been able to catch it
and tomorrow
we shall eat it
in a tasty stew.

TODOS LOS PÁJAROS ANDAN EN UN CONJUNTO DE AMOR

Todos los pájaros andan en un conjunto de amor
buscando comida en febrero.
Todos los árboles botan las hojas,
los pájaros se sientan en las ramas
y se sienten tristes,
no tienen dónde buscar sus gusanos y otros animales
entre las hojas, para alimentarse.
Cuando entra mayo se alegran y abren sus alas,
se saludan, cantan y estiran el pescuezo
mirando los árboles que están coposos de hojas.

Natalia Sequeira

A CONGREGATION OF LOVE

In February all the birds, seeking their food,
unite in a congregation of love.
All the trees shed their leaves,
and the birds perch sadly in the branches,
for there are no leaves where they can seek maggots
and other creatures to feed on.
When May arrives, they perk up and spread their wings,
greet each other, sing, and stretch their necks,
seeing the trees now thick with leaves.

LOS VACUNOS

El ganado corre brinca patea
mientras el sol calienta los campos.
Al llegar la noche
se echan en un solo conjunto
formando un manchón injerto.
Las hembras paridas levantan sus orejas
y olfatean su ternero acariciándolo con la lengua.
Durante las horas profundas de la noche
el adulto rumea los residuos de alimentos
que le quedan en su alargada trompa mientras
descansa de su agotador andar.
Al llegar la madrugada los terneros berrean
en busca de su madre
que a la misma hora tiene la ubre como una enorme pipa
llena de agua,
y los cuatro pezones que le dan su forma como
una importante vasija indígena.
El ternero coloca su fea trompa
acariciando desesperadamente los pezones
henchidos de leche.
Cuando la enorme pipa ya está vacía
a costa de los fuertes chupetazos y golpes
que el ternero le da con su redonda frente,
los tiesos pezones disminuyen
y van quedando como unas pequeñas chuspas
de naranja exprimidas (desjugadas).

Dónald Guevara

CATTLE

The cattle run and skip and stamp about,
while the sun warms the fields.
When night falls
the animals huddle together,
grafted into a dark patchwork.
the cows that have calved twitch their ears
as they smell their calves, caressing them with their tongues.
In the deep hours of the night
the adult beasts chew the cud
in their long snouts
as they rest from the fatigue of movement.
Towards dawn the calves begin to bleat
as they look for their mothers,
who by now have udders like huge barrels filled with water,
and the four teats which give them shape
make them look like heavy Indian jugs.
The calves desperately nuzzle the milk-swollen teats
with their ugly mugs.
When the great barrels have been emptied
by the strenuous butting and sucking
undertaken by the calves' round heads,
the stiff teats shrink
and begin to look like pouches
made of orange skins squeezed dry.

AMOR EN EL CAMPO

Güises que picotean a sus güisas.
Mantis religiosa que se come a sus amados.
Con su ternura los palomos arrullan a sus palomas.
Chicharras que cantan todo el día llamando a sus chicharros.
Quiebra-platas que alumbran en busca de sus amores.
Mariposas que vuelan en sus noches de bodas.
Grillos que cantan largas tonadas para que vengan sus
    amadas.
Sapos que llaman a sus preferidas.
Chayules en grandes ruedas sobre los árboles.
De cuanto amor está lleno el campo.

Elvis Chavarría

LOVE IN THE COUNTRYSIDE

Flycatcher males pecking flycatcher females.
The praying mantis gobbling up her lovers.
Cock-pigeon cooing fondly to hen-pigeon.
She-cicadas singing all day to their he's.
Glow-worms aglow as they seek their loves.
Butterflies on their honeymoon. Crickets
ceaselessly chirruping, beckoning their sweethearts.
Toads calling to their true-loves.
Clouds of gnats wheeling about the trees.
How full of love is the countryside!

FELIZ

Feliz me siento porque tengo a mis padres.
Feliz me siento porque sé leer.
Y feliz me siento porque soy poeta.

Jonny Chavarría
(aged 11)

FAMILY AND FRIENDS

HAPPINESS

I am happy because I have my parents.
I am happy because I can read.
I am happy because I am a poet.

A MI PADRE

Cada vez que te vengo a ver me entristezco.
Me hacen falta tus consejos, las anécdotas
que me platicabas de tus amigos o tuyas.
Ya no te escucho reir alegre.
Sé que estás contento por el gesto que hacés;
te afanás haciendo señas con la mano que te ha quedado buena.
Y cuando no te entiendo, te ponés serio,
mirás para abajo,
y se te rodean los ojos de lágrimas.

Felipe Peña

TO MY FATHER

Each time I come to visit you I am sad.
I miss your wisdom, and the yarns
you told me about your friends, or about yourself.
I no longer hear your cheerful laughter.
Your gestures tell me you are happy.
You strive to signal with your one good hand.
When I don't understand you, you look grave,
eyes downcast,
and glistening with tears.

RECUERDO

No te podría olvidar archipiélago
cuando después que pasaba la lluvia
y quedaba el sol brillante
pasaba Raúl para llevarnos al guabo
a cortar naranjas.
Bajo los verdes oscuros naranjos,
lodazales,
naranjas amarillas picadas por avispas
mierdas de vaca
frescas y viejas.
Yo arriba del palo cortándolas,
Raúl cogiéndolas, la Nubia
echándolas al saco, Lolo
llevándolas al bote y la Myriam
chupándoselas.

Gloria Guevara

A MEMORY

I can never forget you, my chain of islands –
like that time, after the rains,
and in brilliant sunshine,
when Raul came to take us down by the guaba tree
to pick oranges.
Under the dark green orange-trees
deep mud
yellow wasp-bitten oranges
cowpats
new and old.
Me up the tree picking the oranges
Raul gathering them up
Nubia putting them into sacks, Lolo
taking them to the boat and Myriam
just sucking them.

ES CASI YA DE NOCHE

Es casi ya de noche y
el lago está calmo.
Brisas soplan de vez en cuando.
Las garzas pasan a dormir.
Los güises dan sus últimos saltos.
Pero yo estoy solo
viendo a lo lejos
las cordilleras azules de Chontales
y pienso
que a la orilla del lago
está el pequeño pueblo
donde estás vos
Silvia.

Iván Guevara

IT'S ALMOST NIGHT

It's almost night.
The lake is still,
stirred only by a fitful breeze.
Herons are flying to their nests.
Flycatchers dart at the day's last prey.
But I am alone,
gazing at the distant
blue mountains of Chontales,
and thinking
that at the edge of the lake
is the little village
where you are,
Silvia.

EL AMOR ES COMO LA MATA DE FRIJOL

¿Has visto crecer la mata de frijol? Nace, echa hojas, chotes, florece. Y después sólo da frutos y vainas.
Pues así es el amor.

Iván Guevara

LOVE IS LIKE
A BEAN-PLANT

Have you watched a
bean-plant grow? It appears,
puts out leaves, buds, blossoms. Then
later all it does is produce beans
and bean-pods.
Well, that's what love is like.

CON EL PELO ALBOROTADO

Con el pelo alborotado
la blusa abierta y los pies descalzos
estoy acostada sobre una piedra curtida de lama
y mierda de golondrinas.
Y con los ojos fijos mirando la luna a través
de las ramas del roble, pienso en vos Alejandro.

Nubia Arcia

WITH MY HAIR ALL TUMBLED

With my hair all tumbled
my blouse open, barefoot,
I lie on a rock
caked with mud and swallow-droppings.
And as I gaze at the moon
through the branches of the oak-tree
I think of you, Alejandro.

AYER PASÉ POR ESTE RANCHITO

El ranchito estaba sucio
porque es muy temprano;
los niños estaban sucios
porque es muy temprano
y en el forrito viejo y destartalado
estaba una foto de Somoza
porque es muy temprano.

Esperanza Guevara

POLITICS AND REVOLUTION

YESTERDAY I PASSED BY THIS LITTLE HUT

The little hut was dirty –
because it's still very early;

the children were dirty –
because it's still very early;

and on the rickety shelf
was a photo of Somoza –
because it's still very early.

PLAGAS

Las plagas pueden ser naturales o artificiales.
En Solentiname las plagas son
los loros, guatuzas, los zanates, ratones;
zompopos, también hay polillas,
como también hay comerciantes que devoran las cosechas
de los campesinos,
como también patrones que devoran el trabajo de los peones,
igual que los loros, guatuzas, zanates,
ratones, zompopos, devoran el maíz, el arroz, los frijoles.
También las plagas humanas constituyen un sistema de plagas.
Aquí en Solentiname la Compañía ha hecho desaparecer los
    loros,
los ratones, las guatuzas,
que son parte de las plagas que joden al campesino
y creo que la compañía hará desaparecer
la plaga humana, claro que no la compañía del Tránsito
sino la del proletariado.

Felipe Peña

PESTS

Pests may be natural – or they may be artificial.
In Solentiname these are the pests we have:
Parrots, agoutis, grackles, mice;
also *zompopos*, the giant ants. And moths.
Likewise there are traders who devour the harvest
of the peasants,
and there are bosses who devour the labour of the workers,
just as the parrots, agoutis, grackles,
mice and *zompopos*, devour maize, and rice, and beans.
Human pests, too, make up a whole pesty system.
Here in Solentiname the Canal Company has cleared out
      the parrots,
the mice, the agoutis,
which are some of the pests that beset the peasant –
and I think the company will get rid of the human pest –
only of course it won't be the Canal Company,
but the company of the proletariat.

EL PUEBLO EN MISERIA

Llegué a un lugar
donde botan todas
las basuras del pueblo.

Y miré a unos niños
con unos sacos viejos
que los llenaron de tarros oxidados,
zapatos rotos,
pedazos de cajas de cartón viejas.

Y unas moscas se les metían entre los sacos
y se volvían a salir
y se les sentaban en las cabezas.

Gloria Guevara

THE PEOPLE IN POVERTY

I came to a place
where they dump
all the garbage of the town.

And I saw some children
filling a few old sacks
with rusty tins
worn-out shoes
bits of old cardboard boxes.

And some flies crept in among the sacks
and then came out
and settled on the children's heads.

CAMPESINO

El campesino trabaja.
Los ricos ven al pobre sufrir.
Mientras el campesino come frijoles
el rico carne todos los días y
lo que quieran.
El pobre se viste con ropas rajadas
el rico se viste con ropas diolén.
El pobre vive en casas de cartón
y los explotadores se ríen del campesino.

Jonny Chavarría
(aged 11)

PEASANT

The peasant works.
Rich people see poor people suffer.
While the peasant eats beans
rich people eat meat every day and
whatever they want.
Poor people dress in rags,
rich people wear clothes of polyester.
Poor people live in houses made of cardboard,
and the exploiters laugh at the peasant.

SAN CARLOS

El agua cae sobre los techos corroídos.
Una vieja dice: pescado frito, pescado frito.
Perros, gatos, chanchos, en la calle bien sucia.
Un carretón con una campanilla, y un viejo:
a ver, a ver, aquí están los conos.
Cantinas, barberías, billares,
gasolineras, comiderías, putales.
Golondrinas, chayules, moscas, tufo,
mercadeo, más tufo, mercadeo, cagadas,
tufo, Somoza en un afiche cagado de golondrinas.
Cordeles repletos: sábanas, camisas, pantalones, blusas,
el golpe de las mujeres: pon, pa, pon, pa,
lavando, y siguen lavando.
Los mamones, las manzanas, los mangos, el queso, el vajo,
la sandía, el fresco helado, la horchata.
Más mercadeo, más chayules, golondrinas,
más cagadas, más afiches.

Elvis Chavarría

SAN CARLOS

The rain falls on rusty roofs.
An old woman cries out: 'Fried fish! Fried fish!'
Dogs, cats, pigs in the muddy street.
A handcart with a bell, and an old man calling:
'Come along! Come along! Ice cream! Ice cream!'
Snack-bars, barbers' shops, billiard saloons;
petrol-pumps, cafés, whorehouses.
Swallows, midges, flies, stink,
goods for sale, more
stink, more goods, shit, stink, Somoza on a poster
shat on by swallows.
Loaded washing-lines: sheets, shirts, trousers, blouses.
The thud, thud, thud, of women
pummelling the washing, always washing.
Papayas, apples, mangos, cheese, steamed food,
water-melons, iced drinks, barley-water.
More goods, more gnats, more swallows,
more shit, more posters.

LA REVOLUCIÓN ES...

La Revolución es Fidel Castro jugando basket-ball
La Revolución es el Granma donde viajaron los héroes
La Revolución es Sandino diciendo un discurso a su pueblo
La Revolución es que todas las mamás cuiden bien a sus niños
La Revolución es el lago donde hay pescados para todos
La Revolución es una pareja de enamorados
La Revolución es la flor de sacuanjoche
La Revolución es Mario Avila poniéndole música a un poema
La Revolución es una bola de cañón que dispara a los
    imperialistas
La Revolución es vencer a los imperialistas
La Revolución es Ernesto Cardenal escribiendo un poema para
    Solentiname
La Revolución es una mariposa de colores que pasa volando
    alrededor de los héroes
La Revolución son todos los cubanos aplaudiendo a Fidel
La Revolución es mi papá haciendo una escultura con todos sus
    formones.

Juan Agudelo
(aged 7)

THE REVOLUTION IS...

The Revolution is Fidel Castro playing basket-ball
The Revolution is the ship Granma, in which the heroes
    travelled
The Revolution is Sandino making a speech to the people
The Revolution is all mothers looking after their children
    properly
The Revolution is the lake with fish in it for everyone
The Revolution is a pair of lovers
The Revolution is the frangipani flower
The Revolution is Mario Avila setting a poem to music
The Revolution is a shell fired at the imperialists
The Revolution is the defeat of the imperialists
The Revolution is Ernesto Cardenal writing a poem for
    Solentiname
The Revolution is a gaudy butterfly fluttering round the heroes
The Revolution is all the Cubans applauding Fidel
The Revolution is my Dad making a sculpture with all his
    chisels.

BLANCA ESTOY TRISTE

Blanca estoy triste.
Esta tarde no brilla el sol como el de ayer.
La ausencia de vos ha hecho que se apodere de mí
el desespero, el silencio y la melancolía.
Ayer eras vos quien horrorizada
me platicabas cómo los guardias somocistas
asesinaron a tu mamá y a tu hermano William
de quince años
y que los zopilotes allí donde dejaron
los cadáveres bajaban y subían
como aviones que bajan y suben
bombardeando.

Felipe Peña

THE LIBERATION STRUGGLE

I AM SAD, BLANCA

I am sad, Blanca.
Today the afternoon sun does not shine as it did yesterday.
In your absence I have become the prisoner
of despair, and silence, and melancholy.
Yesterday, appalled, you told me
how Somoza's National Guard
had murdered your mother and your brother William,
fifteen years old.
And how, there where they had left the bodies,
the vultures swooped and soared,
like aeroplanes swooping and soaring,
loosing their bombs.

VOS CREÉS

Vos creés que yo no me enamoro
y pensás que soy pendejo porque me hago el que no entiendo
el contenido de tus palabras, el acento de tu voz, la malicia de
 tus miradas.
Posiblemente dudás de tu belleza, por la poca importancia que
 aparento darle,
no quisiera pensar que tenés esa imagen de mí,
te pido que reflexionés y que pensés qué puede
ofrecerte un guerrillero que anda chapoteando lodo
en los caminos de la montaña, durmiendo en tapescos de varas,
o envuelto en un plástico en el suelo. Qué puedo ofrecerte yo
si mi vida se la he ofrecido al pueblo,
no tengo más que la mochila, el fusil, la dotación de tiros
y mi uniforme de verde olivo.

Felipe Peña

YOU SUPPOSE

You suppose I'm not in love with you,
and that I'm mean because I pretend not to understand
the sense of your words, the tone of your voice, the suspicion
 in your looks.
Perhaps you even doubt your own beauty, because I hardly
 seem to notice it.
I don't want you to think of me like that.
Please stop and consider what
a guerrilla fighter can offer you, one who spends his time
wading through mud on mountain paths, sleeping on beds of
 twigs,
or stretched out on a plastic sheet.
What can I offer you
if I have offered my life to the people?
All I have is my pack, my rifle and my ration of bullets,
and my uniform of olive green.

DESPEDIDA DEL PADRE

Me despedí de vos
el lunes 10 de octubre.
Estabas enfermo con la mirada baja.
Me quedaste viendo.
Te prometí volver pronto.
Entrecerraste tus ojos maliciosamente
queriendo decirme: vos no volvés.
Tu cara triste
sentado en el viejo taburete
me echaste el brazo y sin pronunciar palabra
te resignaste a decirme adiós.
Abrazándote por última vez me sonreía
pero mi corazón lloraba.
Sólo yo sabía hacia dónde iba
y por qué te dejaba.

Felipe Peña

FAREWELL TO MY FATHER

I said goodbye to you
on Monday the tenth of October.
You were ill, and your eyes were dull.
You watched me.
I promised to come back soon.
You looked at me warily with half-closed eyes,
meaning to say: You won't come back.

Looking sad
as you sat on the old stool
you put your arms round me
and yielded yourself to our wordless farewell.

As I embraced you for the last time, I was smiling,
but my heart wept.
I alone knew where I was going
and why I was leaving you.

DESPUÉS DE LA EMBOSCADA

Oscurece pronto, comienza a llover y
se borran las pisadas de los guerrilleros.
Hay cansancio en nosotros;
el llano que hay que pasar es grande,
el lodo y el agua nos llegan a la cintura
y ahora todo está oscuro, ni una estrella se ve en el cielo;
la columna camina en silencio.
Sólo un guerrillero piensa escribir un poema.
Sigue lloviendo, los zancudos salen de las yolillas,
el hambre y el sueño es intenso. Me arrecuesto y se
me clavan espinas que entumen mi cuerpo.
No se oyen disparos,
estamos ya cerca del campamento;
se da la orden de descanso. Un compañero,
mientras se fuma un cigarro, me pregunta:
¿es cierto que vos sos poeta?

Iván Guevara

AFTER THE AMBUSH

It soon gets dark. It begins to rain and
the footmarks of the *guerrilleros* are washed away.
We are dog-tired:
the plain that we have to cross is huge.
We are waist-deep in mud and water.
And now all is darkness – not a star to be seen in the sky.
The column advances in silence.
But one *guerrillero* is thinking of writing a poem.
Rain, and more rain. The mosquitoes come out from the
      palm-trees.
Hunger is sharp, sleep is urgent. I lean against a tree
and the thorns spike and numb my body.
No shots are heard,
we are already near our camp;
the order to rest is given. A *compañero*
lights a cigarette, and asks:
Is it true you are a poet?

TENLE MIEDO A LOS POETAS TIRANO

Tenle miedo a los poetas tirano
porque ni con tus tanques sherman
ni con tus aviones a reacción
ni con tu batallón de combate
ni con tu seguridad
ni con tu nicolasa
ni con cuarenta mil marines
ni con tus super-entrenados ránger
ni siquiera tu Dios
evitará que te fusilen en la historia.

Bosco Centeno

WALK IN DREAD OF POETS, TYRANT

Walk in dread of poets, tyrant.
For not your Sherman tanks,
nor your jet planes,
nor your commando battalion,
nor your security forces,
nor your whore Nicolasa,
nor your forty thousand marines,
nor your rangers with their crack training –
none of these –
no, not even your God –
can save you from history's firing-squad.

HERMANO GUARDIA, PERDONÁ

Hermano guardia perdoná que tenga que afinar
bien la puntería al dispararte,
pero de nuestros disparos dependen los hospitales
y las escuelas que no tuvimos,
donde jugarán tus hijos con los nuestros.
Sabé que ellos justificarán nuestros disparos
pero los hechos por vos serán
vergüenza de tu generación.

Bosco Centeno

BROTHER SOLDIER

Soldier of the National Guard, you are my brother,
so you must forgive me if I have to
take careful aim when I shoot you.
But from our bullets will come hospitals
and schools, which we never had before –
schools where your kids will play with our kids.
Take my word, these things will vindicate our killing,
but every shot fired by you will be
the shame of your whole generation.

SUDOROSOS Y ENLODADOS

Sudorosos y enlodados
tres días de marcha y cuatro emboscando
pálidos, con el cuerpo lleno de piquetes
la mochila pesando como una cruz
pasando las postas del campamento despacio,
compañeros con la mirada nos preguntan:
¿Todos completos? Compañero ni un tiro en siete días
nada de contar.
Otros compañeros saldrán mañana a emboscar.

Bosco Centeno

SWEATY AND MUDDY

Sweaty and muddy,
three days marching and four days lying in ambush,
pale, stung all over our bodies,
crucified by the weight of our packs,
slowly we pass the sentries at the camp.
Comrades look at us and their eyes ask:
All present?
Not a shot, *compañeros*, in seven days –
nothing to report.
Tomorrow other *compas* will go out on ambush.

EN LA NOCHE CONFUNDIDOS

En la noche confundidos entre el monte
igual que tigres al acecho
oyéndonos el latido acelerado del corazón
zancudos pasando con ruidos de aviones
no se sienten sus piquetes
el fusil bala en boca, sin seguro
con pulso firme decidido
y pasan sombras de casco y fusil una y otra y otra otra...
y el disparo, seguido de muchos más, callan los sonidos
    de la montaña
y vivas a Sandino a Monimbó
de Patria Libre o Morir
la pólvora que reseca la garganta,
alargándose el tiempo y el silencio roto por
gritos pidiendo clemencia
saliendo de los matorrales siempre al acecho
recogiendo fusiles, documentos
curamos a los guardias heridos
y silenciosos desaparecemos en la montaña.

Bosco Centeno

OBSCURED BY THE NIGHT

Obscured by the night among the scrub,
like tigers lying in wait,
we hear the quickening beat of our hearts.
Mosquitoes hum about us like planes,
but we do not feel their stings.
We carry our guns, loaded, safety catch off,
in firm, decisive hands.
Helmets and rifles pass in profile,
first one, then another, and another, and another...
One shot, then more, many more, extinguish the sounds of the
      mountain.
Then come cries of 'Viva Sandino! Viva Monimbó!
Our country free – or death!'
Our throats are dry with the dust.
Time stretches out and the silence is broken
by cries for mercy.
Still on the alert, we emerge from the thickets,
pick up rifles, documents.
We tend the wounded National Guards
and silently melt into the mountain.

A MIS CUATRO HIJOS EN LA MONTAÑA

Ellos en la montaña
no tienen cobijas
junto a sus compañeros
en el suelo duermen,
el zacate mojado
en las noches de invierno
moja sus cuerpos cansados;
y almuerzo en helicóptero
no les llega
como a la guardia.
Pero ellos con sus vidas
darán a otros en Nicaragua
esas colchas y ese almuerzo.

Olivia Silva

TO MY FOUR SONS IN THE MOUNTAINS

Up there in the mountains
they have no bedding –
with their comrades together
they sleep on the earth.
In the winter nights the wet grass
soaks their weary bodies.
No breakfast is served to them
by helicopter
as it is to the National Guard.
But with their lives
they will bring to others in Nicaragua
both bedding and breakfast.

EL HIJO

Deseo un hijo, y el sentirme ser madre.
Bañarlo todos los días, vestirlo,
perfumarlo, darle su refresco,
y su comida a sus horas.
Contemplarlo, y distinguir a quién se parece
¿a mí o a mi amado?
Soñar que cuando esté grande
sea un combatiente por la liberación del pueblo.

Gloria Guevara

A SON

I long to have a son, and to feel I am a mother;
to bath him each day, to dress him,
to make him smell sweet, to give him his drink
and his food at mealtimes –
to gaze at him, and wonder who he is like – me, or my beloved?
And to dream that when he grows up
he will be a fighter for the freedom of the people.

EL GUERRILLERO

Vos que dejaste el calor de tu hogar
para buscar el amor verdadero.

Si te matan tu muerte no será
en vano
porque vivirás en el recuerdo
del pueblo.

Gloria Guevara

THE GUERRILLERO

You who left the warmth of your home
to look for true love –

If they kill you, your death
will not be in vain
for you will live on
in the memory of the people.

EN NICARAGUA EL GRAN ASALTO

En Nicaragua el gran asalto al cuartel de San Carlos
aquella madruga fría.
El 12 desde la fortaleza miré Solentiname.
El río San Juan corriendo con gamalotes y gallinas
de playa, los patos viajando en una tuca río abajo.
El tiempo pasa como una estrella fugaz.
Iremos hasta la victoria final.
Seremos libres o seremos mártires.

Pedro Pablo Meneses

THE ASSAULT ON SAN CARLOS

IN NICARAGUA THE GREAT ASSAULT

In Nicaragua the great assault on the San Carlos barracks
happened one cold dawn.
On the twelfth I saw Solentiname from the fortress.
There was the River San Juan with flotsam and beach-fowl
      in its current,
and ducks travelling downstream on a piece of driftwood.
Time flashes by like a shooting star.
We shall go on until final victory.
We shall be free or we shall die as martyrs.

12 DE OCTUBRE DE 1977

Son las cuatro. Tenemos que irnos a cruzar el lago.
Olas, viento, más olas.
Al norte quedó Solentiname con frescura
garzas volando al Zacatón
arrozales en corta,
milpas con olor a chilote
pájaros chillones.
Y todo eso, pienso yo,
violado por la G. N.
como violaron a Amada Pineda.

Olivia Silva

THE TWELFTH OF OCTOBER, 1977

It's four o'clock. We must make our way across the lake.
Waves, wind, more waves.
To the north the freshness of Solentiname.
Herons flying to El Zacatón.
Ricefields being cut.
Maizefields smelling of *chilote*,
Shrill bird-song.
And the thought comes to me
that all that has been raped by the National Guard,
just as they raped Amada Pineda.

CUANDO EL ASALTO
AL CUARTEL DE SAN CARLOS

El 12 de octubre entramos al anochecer
al río Guacalito. Gritan los congos al vernos pasar;
yolillas y olor a lodo podrido: nubes
de zancudos pican las caras de los niños.

Mi tensión es nerviosa, solo el canto de los
grillos y el grito del oso-caballo como diciendo:
el pueblo vencerá.

Olivia Silva

AT THE TIME OF THE ASSAULT
ON THE SAN CARLOS BARRACKS

At nightfall on the twelfth of October
we slip into the Guacalito River.
The monkeys howl as they see us pass.
Palm-trees, and the foul stench of sludge.
Clouds of mosquitoes sting the children's faces.

I am tense and nervous. There is only the crickets' song
and the cry of the weird night-bird seeming to say:
The people will win.

CUANDO LOS MUCHACHOS DE SOLENTINAME ASALTARON SAN CARLOS

El botecito azul y blanco
color de cielo y agua
salió del muelle y por última vez
di un vistazo a mi lindo
archipiélago Solentiname.
Aquel caserillito a la orilla
de la costa, algunas
garzas volando bajo el cielo
gris de la tarde, el pato-aguja
comiéndose un pez
debajo de un guabo
el zanate clarinero saltando
los güises, las viudas, y de un
momento a otro ya no vi nada.

Y por fin salimos del lago
entramos al río
hacia Costa Rica.
Anochece, sólo se oye el canto
de los grillos en el silencio
y de nuevo vuelvo
a recordar el canto de
todos los pájaros de Solentiname
como el güis con su güiiis, güiiis
el pijul con su pijul, pijul, pijul y la
viuda.

Y de pronto me despertaron
el pun, pun, pun, el traca
traca de las ametralladoras lejanas.

Elena Pineda

WHEN THE YOUNG MEN AND WOMEN OF SOLENTINAME STORMED SAN CARLOS

The little boat, blue and white,
colour of sky and water,
moved off from the jetty,
and I took a last look
at my lovely Solentiname archipelago:
the tiny house at the edge
of the shore, a few
herons flying beneath the grey
afternoon sky, the needle-billed duck
swallowing a fish,
the grackle with its brassy call
hopping about under a guaba tree,
flycatchers,
and widow-birds –
and all at once I could see nothing more.

And at last we left the lake
and entered the river
on the way to Costa Rica.
Night falls, and all we can hear
is the song of the crickets in the silence –
and I remember again the song
of all the birds in Solentiname,
like the flycatcher *güis* calling *güiiis, güiiis*,
the *pijul* with its cry of *pijul, pijul, pijul* –
and the widow-bird.

And suddenly I was woken
by the pom pom pom
taka taka taka
of distant machine-guns.

RECUERDO AQUELLA MADRUGADA

Recuerdo aquella madrugada de octubre
cuando huíamos de la Guardia Nacional
después del asalto al cuartel de San Carlos
cuando me ahogaba al cruzar el río Frío
y grité: – Me ahogo Iván.

Pero no fue Iván el primero en llegar
sino que fuiste vos Alejandro.

Nubia Arcia

A DAWN MEMORY

I remember that October dawn
when we fled from the National Guard
after the assault on the San Carlos barracks
and I was drowning as we crossed the River Frío
and I yelled: 'I'm drowning, Iván'.

But it wasn't Iván who got there first –
it was you, Alejandro.

AL CHATO MEDRANO, CAÍDO EN EL ASALTO AL CUARTEL DE SAN CARLOS

En aquella madrugada de octubre
de bluyín y chaqueta de azulón
con escopeta de asalto
combatiste junto a nosotros.
Al entrar al viejo cuartel
te hirieron en la pierna derecha;
arrastrándote y con ayuda de un compañero
llegaste hasta nosotros.
Tu cara amplia pero pálida
gritando: – Guarden sus posiciones.

Myriam Guevara

TO CHATO MEDRANO, KILLED IN THE ASSAULT ON THE SAN CARLOS BARRACKS

On that October morning,
dressed in blue jeans and jacket,
carrying an assault gun,
you fought side by side with us.
As you went into the old barracks,
they wounded you in the right leg;
with the help of a *compañero*
you dragged yourself towards us.
Your broad face was pale
as you yelled: 'Stand fast!'

DESPUÉS DEL COMBATE

Son las seis de la tarde.
Me siento con fiebre.
Comienza a llover en
gotas grandes y seguidas.
Corto dos hojas
verdes y redondas
las pongo en mi cabeza.
Cerca de nosotros
se ven las luces de Los Chiles.

Myriam Guevara

AFTER THE BATTLE

It's six in the evening.
I think I have a temperature.
A steady rain begins to fall
in huge drops.
I cut two round green leaves
and put them on my head.
Quite near to us
we can see the lights of Los Chiles.

EN SOLENTINAME

En Solentiname allí no ha quedado nada;
no está Ernesto dialogando el Evangelio
con nosotros. Terminó aquel almuerzo en familia.

No está Ernesto dirigiendo las pinturas en Solentiname.
Sólo el canto de los pájaros ha quedado
y la presencia repugnante de la guardia de Somoza.

Olivia Silva

CAPTIVITY AND EXILE

IN SOLENTINAME

In Solentiname there is nothing left.
There is no Ernesto chewing over the gospels with us –
the family lunch is over.

Nor is Ernesto guiding the artists
at work on their paintings in Solentiname.
Only the song of the birds has remained,
and the loathsome presence of Somoza's guards.

A MI NICARAGUA DESDE EL EXILIO

Nicaragua, llora Nicaragua como muchacha dejada,
llora Nicaragua. Pero no está lejos el día
en que ya no tengamos que vivir en la clandestinidad o el exilio
ni circulen papeletas y documentos clandestinos.
Llegará el día en que resuciten miles de héroes
aún ignorados por el pueblo.
Llegará el día en que podamos gritar en plena calle
VIVA EL FRENTE SANDINISTA.

Iván Guevara

TO MY NICARAGUA, FROM EXILE

Nicaragua is weeping, weeping like a forsaken girl.
Nicaragua is weeping... But the day is near
when we shall no longer have to live in hiding or in exile,
or distribute leaflets and documents secretly.
The day will come when thousands of heroes will rise up
who are as yet unknown to the people.
The day will come when we shall be able to shout
in the open street:
LONG LIVE THE SANDINISTA FRONT!

EN SOLENTINAME

Todo quedó allá en Solentiname: el lago las
islas la iglesia donde nos reuníamos todos
los domingos, los árboles de aguacate que
están junto a la plaza donde jugábamos fútbol,
las tardes con el lago calmo o levemente
interrumpido por algún aletazo de un tiburón
o de un güis que se baña, las noches de luna
cuando jugábamos o bailábamos con las hermanas
de la Nubia, y mi guitarra con que tocaba y cantaba
algunas canciones de Silvio Rodríguez
o de Carlos Mejía.
Ya no volveremos a ver a Ernesto bajar de
su casa al muelle con el maletín su capote el
sombrero y algún libro en la mano para ir
a celebrar misa a Papaturro.

Iván Guevara

IN SOLENTINAME

We have left everything behind in Solentiname: the lake,
the islands, the church where we all met
every Sunday, the avocado trees next
to the square where we played football,
the afternoons when the lake was calm, or
lightly ruffled by a shark's fin
or a flycatcher having a bath: the moonlit nights
when we played or danced
with Nubia's sisters,
with me playing my guitar and singing
songs by Silvio Rodríguez
or Carlos Mejía.
We shall never again see Ernesto coming down
from his house to the jetty, with his bag and
his cloak and hat and a book in his hand, on the way
to celebrate mass in Papaturro.

LA IGLESIA SOLA

Está sola la iglesia ahora
sin el grito de los niños
o el sonar de guitarras.
Ahora sólo la naturaleza da cuenta de eso.
Volverá a crecer la hierba como en un principio,
el viento y la lluvia azotarán la palmera florecida
llegarán los pájaros a comer mangos,
las golondrinas seguirán haciendo sus nidos
en los aleros de la iglesia.
Ahora sólo las flores y el canto de los pájaros
alegrarán allí en los días de silencio.

Iván Guevara

THE EMPTY CHURCH

The church is empty now:
no children yelling,
no guitars strumming.
Nature alone takes note of what is happening there.
The grass will grow again as before,
the wind and the rain will lash the flowering palm-tree,
birds will come and eat mangos,
swallows will still build their nests
in the eaves of the church.
Now only the flowers and the song of the birds
can bring joy in the silent days.

VISITA DE UNA AMIGA

Ayer viniste sorpresivamente
te sentaste viendo para la celda
nunca imaginé que vinieras a verme
sin importarte la humillación que te hicieron los guardias.
Hoy no te importó la lluvia
prometiste que venías y viniste.
Todo lo que sufra en la cárcel se me olvidará
pero tus miradas tus palabras
y el beso de despedida no lo olvidaré Cristina.

Felipe Peña

VISIT FROM A FRIEND

Yesterday you surprised me with a visit.
You sat looking into the cell.
I never dreamed you would come to see me,
heedless of the guards and their base treatment of you.
Today you didn't even feel the rain.
You promised to come, and you came.
Whatever I may suffer in prison, I shall forget.
But your looks, and your words, and the farewell kiss,
these I shall not forget, Cristina.

NOSTALGIA DESDE LA CÁRCEL

Después de cuatro meses de no ver el sol,
por primera vez a las 2 de la tarde el cabo de guardia
abrió el candado de La Bartolina: Felipe, vas a picar leña, salí.
Como la zorra de su cueva viendo para todos lados
desesperado quedé viendo la playa al frente
las manchas azules son las islas de Solentiname
y las lanchas alejándose poco a poco rumbo a Granada
y me hice la ilusión de viajar un día
a mis islas amadas o a Granada.

Felipe Peña

HOMESICKNESS IN PRISON

After four months with no sight of the sun,
one afternoon at two o'clock the captain of the guard
for the first time unlocked the door of La Bartolina prison.
'Felipe, you're going to chop wood. Out you go!'
Like a fox peering out from his lair in all directions,
I stared hopelessly at the beach in front of me,
at the blue shapes of the islands of Solentiname,
at the little boats making their slow way towards Granada;
and I had a vision that I might one day travel
to my beloved islands, or to Granada.

A ESPERANZA MI MUJER

La luna que se filtra entre las ramas de la montaña
y se refleja en la champa, me trae tu recuerdo.
Pienso que en San José entre luces de Navidad
apenas verás esta luna hermosa como la revolución,
o que tal vez nuestras miradas estén juntas
en algún lugar del cielo
o tal vez estés llorando al recordarme sin saber
si estoy vivo,
y nuestras hijas estarán jugando
a las señoras, con tus zapatos en la sala
Vos comprendés, amor, que nuestra pena
en este momento histórico es una satisfacción.

Bosco Centeno

★   ★   ★

Todo será distinto cuando triunfe la revolución.
El amor al pueblo será nuestro amor.
Pero nosotros dos nos amaremos lo mismo.

Bosco Centeno

TO MY WIFE, ESPERANZA

The moonlight, filtered through the branches of the mountain
 forest,
dappling the earth below, brings you to mind.
I think that among the Christmas lights in San José
you will scarcely see this moon, bright as the revolution;
or that perhaps our eyes will meet
somewhere in the sky;
or perhaps you are weeping as you remember me, not knowing
if I am alive;
and our little girls will be wearing your shoes
and playing at being ladies in the living-room.
I know that you understand, my love, that
in this historic moment our grief is a fulfilment.

★ ★ ★

Everything will change after the revolution.
Our love will be love for the people.
But we shall love each other just the same.

SOLENTINAME

Solentiname fue Julio Guevara con su vara de madroño y su risa,
sacando peces del lago.
Fue las muchachas arregladitas en sus botes de remos, como ramos de flores
yendo a misa.
Y las garzas en la costa que como dice Alejandro: De lejos se pueden
confundir con una virgen.
Y las fiestas con los tragos bajo los palos de mango frente a la iglesia con el tocadisco de Chono.
Fue el pueblo discutiendo el evangelio los domingos.
Y las idas a coger tortugas y garrobos para nuestros almuerzos comunales.
Y la música de Elvis, William y Adancito los domingos.
Y la bulla de los niños en los botes en camino de la escuela ahuyentando
patos que se levantaban cagando.
Solentiname fue nuestro juramento de Patria Libre o Morir.
Y Ernesto profetizando tiempos y tierras nuevas.
Y la Compañía monopolizando las tierras.
Y los cuadros llenos de vida de los pintores campesinos.
Solentiname es Julio Guevara en el exilio con su sonrisa entreviendo el futuro.
Es Elvis y Dónald, presos con la capucha ensangrentada arpillados como
sacos en una lancha y llevados a Managua (no hemos vuelto a saber de ellos).
Es Felipe preso en San Carlos, como una chorcha en jaula sin poder escribir.
Es el domingo como un día más.

SOLENTINAME

Solentiname used to mean: Julio Guevara with his arbutus
	fishing-rod, and his laughter,
hauling fish from the lake.
It meant neat little girls in their rowing-boats, like bunches of
	flowers,
going to mass.
And the herons on the shore which, as Alejandro puts it, from a
	distance
might be mistaken for statues of the Virgin.
And drinking-parties with Chono's gramophone
under the mango trees opposite the church.
It meant the people discussing the gospels on a Sunday.
And outings to catch tortoises and lizards for our communal
	lunches.
And on Sundays, too, the music of Elvis, William and little
	Adam.
And the clamour of the kids in boats on their way to school,
scaring the ducks, which scatter their droppings as they take to
	the air.
Solentiname was our oath: Our country free – or death!
And Ernesto prophesying new times and new lands.
And the Canal Company grabbing all the land.
And lively groups of peasant painters.
Solentiname now means: Julio Guevara in exile, smilingly
	glimpsing the future.
It means Elvis and Dónald, prisoners, their hooded heads
	bloody,
trussed up and bundled into a boat and taken to Managua (no
	news of them since).
It means Felipe, captive in San Carlos, like a caged woodcock,
	not even able to write.
It means Sunday – now just a day like any other.

Es José y Oscar torturados por el ránger Franklin Montenegro.
Es el recuerdo de nuestras islas.
(Es la garza en la costa que de lejos se puede confundir con una
 virgen).
Es nuestras casas donde saciaron su rabia de prepotentes
 impotentes.
Es los niños en las casas porque no hay escuelas.
Es el dolor que hay que tener para dar vida.
Solentiname será Julio Guevara con su risa y los nietos sacando
 peces
del lago.
Y las garzas de lejos semejando vírgenes.
Y los gritos de los niños espantando patos cagones
en camino para la escuela de la revolución.
Y las tierras de la Compañía convertidas en cooperativas
 ganaderas.
Y el sí compañero machetero, y sí compañero campisto, sí
 compañero.
Cada día será un domingo y una misa.
Será
    Será
        Será
            será a cada uno según sus necesidades.

Bosco Centeno

It means José and Oscar, tortured by the ranger Franklin
      Montenegro.
It means the memory of our islands –
the heron on the shore that from afar could be mistaken for a
      statue of the Virgin –
our houses, where those supertyrants vented their impotent
      fury –
the children who stay at home because there are no schools –
the pain that goes with giving birth.
Solentiname *will* mean: Julio Guevara with his laughter, and his
      grandchildren
hauling fish from the lake.
And herons that from a distance look like statues of the Virgin.
And the cries of children shit-scaring the ducks
as they make their way to the school of the revolution.
And the lands of the Canal Company converted to cooperative
      cattle-ranches.
And yes, *compañero* plantation-worker, yes *compañero* cowherd,
      yes, *compañero* –
Every day will be Sunday, with a mass.
And it will be
      it will be
            it will be
                  it will be – to each according to his need.

INDEX OF POETS

Juan Agudelo (aged 7): Flyleaf, 14, 62
Nubia Arcia: 50, 94
Bosco Centeno: 26, 32, 72, 74, 76, 78, 112, 114
Eddy Chavarría: 16, 22, 28
Elvis Chavarría: 8, 18, 22, 24, 38, 60
Jonny Chavarría (aged 11): 40, 58
Alejandro Guevara: 30
Dónald Guevara: 10, 36
Esperanza Guevara: 52
Gloria Guevara: 44, 56, 82, 84
Iván Guevara: 46, 48, 70, 102, 104, 106
Myriam Guevara: 96, 98
Pedro Pablo Meneses: 12, 20, 86
Felipe Peña: 42, 54, 64, 66, 68, 108, 110
Elena Pineda: 92
Natalia Sequeira: 34,
Olivia Silva: 80, 88, 90, 100

NOTES

The word Solentiname has five syllables in Spanish with the stress on the penultimate. It is pronounced approximately Sol-en-ti-náh-may.

There are two seasons in Nicaragua: the rainy season called winter, from about May till October and the dry season called summer, from November to April.

The illustrations to the section titles show (1) a freshwater shark (found only in Lake Nicaragua); (2) a flame-tree (*malinche*, Latin: *delonix regia*); (3) heron; (4) orange picking (*A Memory*); (5) a giant ant (*zompopo*); (6) Felipe Peña in combat gear; (7) ducks on driftwood with shooting star (*In Nicaragua the Great Assault*); (8) Felipe Peña in prison. The two drawings of Felipe Peña are copied from photos reproduced in *El Asalto a San Carlos, Testimonios de Solentiname* (Managua 1986).